*In loving memory of my grandfather,
Willie Harris, Sr.*

*You've always believed in me as a writer.
Now it's a reality.*

# ONE STEP AT A TIME

Danika K. Frank

*One Step at A Time*

Copyright ©2021 Danika K. Frank

All rights reserved.

ISBN: 978-1-955579-00-1

No part of this book may be reproduced or transmitted in any form or by any means, electronic or mechanical, including photocopying, recording, or by any information storage and retrieval system without express written permission of the publisher, except in the case of brief quotations embodied in critical reviews and certain non-commercial uses permitted by copyright law.

All Scripture references are from the King James Version (NKJV) Bible unless otherwise noted.

This book contains material protected under International and Federal Copyright Laws and Treaties. Any unauthorized reprint or use of this material is prohibited.

Publishing in the United States of America

Publisher: Luminous Publishing
www.luminouspublishing.com

For bulk orders or other inquiries, email:
info@luminouspublishing.com

# Table of Contents

Acknowledgements .......................................... vi
Introduction ................................................... 2
Chapter 1: Honesty ........................................ 8
Chapter 2: Hope ............................................ 21
Chapter 3: Trust in God ................................ 33
Chapter 4: Truth ............................................ 44
Chapter 5: Confession .................................. 57
Chapter 6: Change of Heart ......................... 68
Chapter 7: Humility ...................................... 81
Chapter 8: Seeking Forgiveness .................. 90
Chapter 9: Restitution and Reconciliation ... 100
Chapter 10: Daily Accountability ................. 109
Chapter 11: Personal Revelation ................. 119
Chapter 12: Service ...................................... 127
Conclusion .................................................... 139

# Acknowledgements

# One Step at a Time: Acknowledgements

I first want to thank my Lord and Savior, Jesus Christ, for all the grace and mercy bestowed upon me to complete this book and see it through. It came with some challenges, but by His grace, it became a reality.

Secondly, I would like to thank my wonderful and supportive husband for believing in me and my dreams and for pushing and encouraging me when I doubted myself. To my amazing sons, Elijah and Noah, thanks for being an inspiration and daily reminder that it is not about me!

Lastly, I want to thank my family, friends, spiritual parents, and church family for all the words of encouragement, support, help, and prayers! I really couldn't have done it without you all.

A special thanks to Karolyne Roberts and Luminous Publishing for such an amazing platform and ministry to help aspiring authors complete and publish their work.

# Introduction

# ONE STEP AT A TIME: INTRODUCTION

*"Hi, my name is Danika, and I am an addict."*

You know, it's funny saying that because I really mean it. Me being an addict may not necessarily be in the sense of how it is considered in Alcoholics Anonymous (AA), Narcotics Anonymous (NA), Gamblers Anonymous (GA), or the like, but it holds just about the same weight as those who state their name in meetings and share their stories.

At meetings, when an individual stands up and states their name followed by "and I'm an addict/alcoholic," that individual is confessing that his/her life has been unmanageable and controlled by a substance. Before receiving Jesus Christ as my Lord and Savior in 2013, I saw how my life was unmanageable and controlled by alcohol, lies, sex, and clubbing. I related to those individuals who uttered those words, even when shame laced their voice, and shared their stories because I've walked in similar shoes. I'd be lying if I said that I wasn't blessed by AA/NA meetings, from hearing individuals share their stories.

### *Recovery = Renewing*

Alcoholics Anonymous, Narcotics Anonymous, Gamblers Anonymous, and other similar meetings are like church and ministry. What I mean is, each day, we tell our story and share our testimony and speak life into other individuals; we are saying, "Hi, my name is (your name here), and I am an addict" who is in recovery because we all are addicts! *"All have sinned and fall short of the glory of God."*[1]

There is a story behind every Christian where they were once in bondage to sin (addiction), and the Lord set them free once they accepted Him as Lord and Savior over their lives; otherwise, there would have been no reason for a Savior, if we didn't need saving, now would there? So yes, even Christians were once addicts freed from bondage.

While sitting in a meeting, I received a revelation. Before Christ (BC), we all had our "thing." It could have been sex, drugs, alcohol, shopping, stealing, stripping, dealing, whatever! We all had something! And every time we tell our story, we share how we have been delivered, cleansed, and made whole!

Now you may be wondering, "How can you incorporate God into that?" Good question! I recall sitting in church one day, hearing Pastor Tracy Casby, Sr., of Full Life Faith Ministries, say, "Look for God in every

---

[1] Romans 3:23

situation," and that is exactly what I did! While sitting in a meeting one night, I began to pray and ask God to reveal His purpose to me. I asked, "Lord, why am I here? What can I learn and take from being here in this meeting?" It was then, sitting in a meeting when I conceived this book.

God showed me how the 12 Steps of Recovery can be applied to our everyday lives and how each step is uniquely designed to not only help the addict recover, but they can also help the sinner live right. Now, I am not saying this book, or the 12 Steps replace the Word of God, nothing can do that. God's Word is true, and it will still stand when everything else falls. However, these steps can be utilized as a tool in our Christian Journey. Not only that, but I have also noticed that during these meetings, God is talked about often and I do believe that recovery is a God thing; because honestly, what can we do without God? NOTHING, NO THING, NOT a THING!

**Recovery.**

I was thinking about the word "recovery" and why it was selected to define the solution to addiction. I first looked up the meaning of the prefix "re-," and dictionary.com says, "*re-* is used with the meaning 'again' or 'again and again' to indicate repetition," and then I thought about the word "cover."

When I think about something being covered, I think about something being protected. You cover your mouth when you sneeze or cough to protect others from receiving your germs and becoming sick. You cover your body with a blanket to protect yourself from the cold. You cover a wound to protect it from becoming infected. Not to mention, Jesus shed His blood on the cross to cover us and protect us from death, if we choose to believe in Him. *"For without the shedding of the blood, there is no remission/forgiveness,"* and without forgiveness of sins, we are sentenced to death. *"For the wages of sin is death."* (See John 3:16, Hebrews 9:22, and Romans 6:23).

After thinking about that, it dawned on me why "Recovery" is so important.

Recovery = Renewing.

Recovery for an addict is what Renewing is for a believer. In Recovery, we are protecting ourselves from addiction again and again by working the steps of recovery daily. Not only are we protecting ourselves, but we are also recovering what addiction took away from us.

## One Step at a Time: Introduction

That could be health, relationships, faith, and so on. Likewise, after being born again, we must continually renew our minds[2] to stay as far away from sin and walk in our newness of life. In addition to that, God will restore.[3]

### *We all are addicts!*

Now, let us begin our journey, one step at a time. Remembering, as they say in recovery groups, *"It only works if you work it!"*

---

[2] Romans 12:2

[3] 1 Peter 5:10

# Chapter 1:
## Honesty

> Honesty: "Admit that you, of yourself, are powerless to overcome your addictions and that your life has become unmanageable."[4]

*"If we say that we have no sin, we deceive ourselves, and the truth is not in us. If we confess our sins, He is faithful and just to forgive us our sins and to cleanse us from all unrighteousness." - 1 John 1:8-9*

The first step in the Addiction Recovery Model is honesty. Addicts are to admit that they, of themselves, are powerless to overcome their addictions and their life has become unmanageable. This is what we are to do when coming to Christ. Our addictions are sins, and we have to be honest and admit that we are sinners in need of a Savior! Romans 5:6 says, *"For when we were still without strength, in due time Christ died for the ungodly."*

Without God, we are ungodly, and without His strength, we are weak. Therefore, we do not have the power or the strength to overcome our addictions or strongholds.

---

[4] The Church of Jesus Christ of Latter-Day Saints. (2012). Addiction Recovery Model. Retrieved by http://addictionrecovery.lds.org/steps/1?lang=eng

Since we cannot overcome the addictions, they take over our lives, and our lives become unmanageable.

*Addictions are your god.*

**The Merriam-Webster Dictionary defines addiction as:**

1. A strong and harmful need to regularly have something or do something

2. An unusually great interest in something or a need to do or have something

**The medical definition of addiction is:**

1. Compulsive physiological need for and use of a habit-forming substance (as heroin, nicotine, or alcohol) characterized by tolerance and by well-defined physiological symptoms upon withdrawal

2. Persistent compulsive use of a substance known by the user to be physically, psychologically, or socially harmful[5]

---

[5] Merriam-Webster Dictionary. (2015). Retrieved from http://www.merriam-webster.com/dictionary/addiction

If not all, most of us have our addictions even though some are not as noticeable. Addictions are typically only associated with drugs or alcohol, so when it's something else (sex, shopping, social media, gambling, etc.), we may feel it's okay. By us generalizing and only categorizing drugs and alcohol as addictions, we tend to feel like we don't have addictions and justify the other things (sex, shopping, etc.) saying, "Well, it's not drugs or alcohol, so it's alright." This, my brothers and sisters, is a trick of the enemy! If the "other thing" is making your life unmanageable, it is an addiction.

There is God's justification, and then there is ours. *"For all have sinned and fall short of the glory of God, being justified freely by His grace through the redemption that is in Christ Jesus."*[6] When God justifies us, He does it through faith and by the righteousness of Christ, and He allows us to be "just" even though naturally, we are all sinners. However, when we allow the enemy to use us, and we justify things and ourselves, we try to make our wrongs right even though they're still wrong.

For example, you are on a job, and the job purchases supplies for you; they are your supplies while you are on the job, but then you leave the job for whatever reason, and you

---

[6] Romans 3:23-24

take the supplies with you. My friend, you just stole supplies. We justify the theft by saying, "They purchased it for me, so technically it's mine," which is true, but "technically" it became theirs again the moment you stopped working there. And that is how the enemy causes us to use justification to allow ourselves to think stealing is right when it is wrong. Remember the commandment: "*Thou shalt not steal?*"[7] No? Well, no worries, now you know. You're welcome.

Another example: You are married, and you have obtained a new friend of the opposite sex that your spouse doesn't know about (RED FLAG!) or you have an old friend of the opposite sex and your spouse knows about them. Well, one day, you noticed something changed within yourself toward that friend and the conversations shift from a friendly "How you doing?" to a 2 a.m. "What you doing?" (and don't act like you don't know what I mean!)

Even if you hadn't "technically" gone through with the act of adultery, the moment those conversations shifted, and you began to lust after that other person; you, my friend,

---

[7] Exodus 20:15

have already committed adultery in your heart (Matthew 5:28) and we know *"as a man thinks in his heart, so is he."*[8]

Those are only two of many ways we justify things the wrong way. Since we are working on honesty, I'm sure if we are truly honest with ourselves, we can come up with other ways we have justified something wrong to make it seem right. If we do something one too many times, it can become a habit. One thing I have learned about habits is that they are easy to form but hard to break. Habits then turn into addictions, and once that happens, we will find ourselves back in this place again.

We now know just about anything can be an addiction. Sex, drugs, working, alcohol, Facebook, Instagram, Pinterest, *Scandal, The Walking Dead,* football, working out, school, gambling, sleeping, and the list goes on. A few years back, I promise you; I could have been a moderator for Facebook Anonymous! I was addicted to Facebook, according to those definitions. I HAD to have it!

I couldn't go a day, a second, without being on Facebook. That could have been me posting or scrolling – I had to see that screen! I would ignore people, tell them to "hold up while I post this," update my status to post my life

---

[8] Proverbs 23:7

second by second, wake up and check Facebook, take a leak and scroll down my Newsfeed, be at work sneaking a peek, and you couldn't tell me anything! Five minutes without Facebook was TORTURE!

> If God calls you to spend time with Him, are you going to do five more finger strokes, two more board pins, watch thirty more seconds of that show, and/or twenty more minutes in that conversation?

I would get all anxious and worked up, my palms would start sweating, or I would start to itch – going through withdrawals because I didn't have that blue square with the white "F" in my face. How many of you know that is a problem? That is an addiction.

**God says this:**

*"I am the Lord your God, who brought you out of the land of Egypt, out of the house of bondage. You shall have no other gods before me...you shall not bow down to them nor serve them. For I, the Lord your God, am a jealous God, visiting the iniquity of the fathers upon the children to the third and fourth generations of those who hate Me, but*

*showing mercy to thousands, to those who love Me and keep My commandments."*[9]

Addictions are your god. Whatever you are addicted to is what controls you and has power over you. When you indulge and give into that addiction, you are bowing down to and serving that addiction. You allow that addiction to have precedent in your life and you are telling the addiction, *"I am yours, and I will follow you wherever you may go."*

These are the things that we must come to terms with to successfully accomplish step one of the 12 Steps of Recovery. Step one is honesty; so, let us be honest with ourselves.

## Look back at those definitions and ask yourself the following questions:

1. Do I have a strong and harmful need or interest to have something or do something regularly?

2. Do I have a constant need for a habit that if this habit does not happen, I will begin to have withdrawals?

---

[9] Exodus 20:2-3; 5-6

If the answer is "Yes" to any one of those questions or any part; then you are in luck! On the other hand, if you are thinking, "It's strong but not harmful" or "I'm okay if I go a few days without it; I don't have withdrawals;" then let us dive a little deeper.

***Another reality we must be honest about is that our life is not ours, so it is not to be managed by us.***

Remember, we said addictions are your god, and God says there should be no other gods before Him, so let's evaluate this further. Does this "possible" addiction you are thinking of come before God? What I mean is, if He calls you to spend time with Him, are you going to do five more finger strokes on Facebook, Twitter, or Instagram, two more board pins on Pinterest, watch thirty more seconds of that show, and stay twenty more minutes in that conversation?

The definition of <u>unmanageable</u> is "difficult or impossible to manage or control, difficult to carry or maneuver; unwieldy."[10] An unmanageable life is what happens when we find ourselves in active addiction.

When our addictions take over us, we lose control and power, and the addictions manage our lives. Our addictions become the author of our lives: adding, deleting, and rewording as they please. Our addictions even begin to control our emotions and our actions; telling us what and how to feel, think, and react. Dear friend: An unmanageable life is not life.

Furthermore, another reality we must be honest about is that our life is not our own, so it is not to be managed by us. You see, Jesus gave His life for ours – a Life for a life.

> **An unmanageable life is not life.**

*"Then He said to them all, 'If anyone desires to come after Me, let him deny himself, and take up his cross daily, and follow Me.'"*[11] In return, as believers, we give our lives back to Him.

Realizing that we, of ourselves, are powerless

---

[10] Unmanageable. (n.d.) *American Heritage® Dictionary of the English Language, Fifth Edition.* (2011). Retrieved from http://www.thefreedictionary.com/unmanageable

[11] Luke 9:23

over our addictions, we allow God the opportunity to take reign.

Additionally, God will order your steps during this 12-step program to overcoming your addictions and sins. How do I know this? The Bible tells us that *"the steps of a good man are ordered by the Lord"*[12], not by addictions and not by us.

> So honestly, what are your addictions?
>
> Take a moment and think about it. Have an honesty hour/moment with yourself and write down all of your addictions. I guarantee you have some, however, if you find yourself struggling to write something down, pray and ask the Lord to reveal to you what your addictions are. After all, since we justify things, what we think is/was right just may be wrong. Once you have identified your addictions, ask yourself, "Is my life unmanageable because of these?"

If your life is unmanageable because of your addictions, then there is great news! Once we take that first step of

---

[12] Psalm 37:23

honesty and admit that we, of ourselves, are powerless to overcome our addictions and that our lives have become unmanageable, we can begin to move on to step number two: Hope.

*"When I took a look at myself, I knew I needed to be changed."* -Anonymous

## Chapter 2:

*Hope*

Hope: "Come to believe that the power of God can restore you to complete spiritual health."[4]

*"Now may the God of peace Himself sanctify you completely; and may your whole spirit, soul, and body be preserved blameless at the coming of our Lord Jesus Christ. He who calls you is faithful, who also will do it." - 1 Thessalonians 5:8*

The second step of recovery is hope. We have to come to believe that the power of God can restore us to complete spiritual health, which it can! Hope is something that you cannot buy; however, I believe it can sometimes be hard to attain. When things are constantly going bad, or it seems as if we are failing and falling into the same thing(s) over and over again, we tend to lose hope.

**Hope is a part of recovery, so you have to have hope in order to recover!**

For me, before Christ (BC), not only was Facebook an addiction, but men were as well. And not just any man but taken men – married men, men in relationships, even men who have dated my friends. From continually falling for, hooking up with, and messing around with the same type of dudes, I lost hope. I lost hope knowing that, if I continued down that path, I would never have a mutually exclusive relationship.

Deep down, I always wanted to be a wife and have a family with my own husband; however, I lost hope in that because I couldn't see it happening with the way I was living my life. Then, faith came in, and God stepped in! I became honest with myself, admitting that I could not manage my own life (step one). Then, there was hope, and God restored me to complete spiritual health (step two)! I'm happily married now! The words "hope," "believe," and "faith," I believe, go hand in hand.

**Merriam-Webster Dictionary defines the three as follows:**

## Hope

1. To cherish a desire with anticipation
2. To desire with expectation of obtainment
3. To expect with confidence

## Believe

1. To accept something as true, genuine, or real
2. To have a firm conviction as to the goodness, efficacy, or ability of something
3. To hold an opinion as an opinion
4. To consider to be true or honest or regard something as true.

## Faith

1. Sincerity of intentions
2. Firm belief in something which there is no proof, complete trust
3. Something that is believed especially with strong conviction[5]

Biblically, the definition of faith is: "*the substance of things hoped for, the evidence of things not seen.*"[13]

> What is something that you feel hopeless about? What addiction(s) do you keep giving into time after time that is making you feel like you have no hope and will forever remain incomplete? Have you thought about it? Do you have it in your head? Okay now, write it down and throw it away because it no longer exists! Hope is a part of recovery, so you have to have it in order to recover!

Our addictions tend to take away our hope and our trust goes from God to whatever we are consumed by, but there is hope, and in that hope, there is restoration. Don't believe me? Let's ask our friend Job.

Job was an addict. His addiction was God. He was so caught up and strung out on God that God pretty much threw him out there for Satan to attack. God asked Satan, "Have you considered My servant Job?"[14] and the Lord allowed Satan to attack him, but Satan could not lay a hand on Job (Job 1:12). Satan went on to attack Job and take away everything that Job possessed: his property, his children, and even his health.

**Addictions will cause you to lose things.**

In the midst of losing all of his possessions and his body being covered from head to toe with painful boils, Job started to lose hope. In Job chapter 3, he cursed the day he was born, and from there, his friends along with his wife began to question his integrity and his life.

Listen. Be careful of who is in your ear and around you while you are going through various trials and tribulations. A person cannot understand something they, themselves, cannot personally attest to. This is why meetings, Bible study, and church are important!

---

[13] **Hebrews 11:1**

[14] **Job 1:8**

At meetings, Bible study, and church, you are surrounded by a community of individuals who can relate. Therefore, when you share what you are going through, they can support and encourage you because they can empathize with you. Before realizing I had an addiction to certain things and before studying about addictions and mental health, I thought it was easy to get over something or to stop doing something. I thought all a person had to do was stop until I found myself deep in my sins and addictions, then I realized for myself that it is not that easy!

Now, I don't want to taint the story of Job, because it truly is a beautiful story. Although God was his addiction, it seemed to have gotten him in trouble given the fact that he lost all of his possessions and his body covered in boils. However, when we get to the end of Job 42, we see step two being worked. Job worked step one and became honest with himself. He also repented to God, and God restored him to complete spiritual health. The latter part of Job 42:10 says, "Indeed the Lord gave Job twice as much as he had before." TWICE! Job got double for his trouble! Does that not give you hope!

Although our addictions, our sins, cause us to lose things in life and push us further away from God, we must always keep in mind that without Him, we are not strong enough to say "no" to whatever is holding and keeping us.

The Bible Says *"I can do **all** things through Christ who strengthens me,"*[15] therefore, with Him, you and I can, and we will overcome our addictions!

I mentioned earlier about meetings, Bible study, and church being important, and they are. This 12-step model is said to work only if you work it. As you continue to attend meetings, Bible study, church, and surround yourself with like-minded people, hear the stories of how others overcame, and more; hope starts to rise up on the inside of you.

Our brother James says to *"confess your faults one to another...that ye may be healed,"*[16] not in a sense of running your mouth and telling everyone your business, but to help others and let them know they are not alone. People need to know that, as Christians, most importantly, we are not perfect and there are some things that we deal and struggle with. However, when we allow God to be God and do a work in, with, and through us, our addictions and our sin will no longer control us. How are others supposed to know there is hope and they can overcome if we don't open up about our addictions and share our stories and testimonies?

---

[15] Philippians 4:13

[16] James 5:16a

## ONE STEP AT A TIME: HOPE

*How about, through you, you let others see and believe.*

The reason I believe most people are not fully committed to Christ and the 12-Step Program to recovery and the reason we tend to run away, stop going to church/meetings, and do our own thing is because we are a people of "let me see." There is a story in the Bible, in the latter part of John 20, about a man named Thomas.

Thomas was one of the twelve disciples, and when Jesus rose from the dead, He went to visit the disciples. When Jesus went to them the first time, Thomas was not present; however, the other disciples told Thomas they had seen Jesus. Thomas didn't believe them and told them in verse 25, *"Unless I see in His hands the print of the nails, and put my finger into the print of the nails, and put my hand into His side, I will not believe."*

In other words, Thomas was like, "Whatever bruh. I saw Him die and not rise, so I'm not 'bout to believe nothing y'all say unless I see it for myself." Well, Jesus came back eight days later to visit with the disciples again, and He told Thomas to do as he said. So Thomas did, putting his finger into the print of the nails and his hand into Jesus' side and Thomas believed. However, Jesus wasn't having it because He knows how we humans are and He knew that He would no longer be present in the flesh where we could naturally "see" Him and believe. He said: *"Thomas, because you have seen Me, you have believed. Blessed are those who have not seen and yet have believed."*[17] How about, through you, dear reader, you let others see and believe.

This is why this step is very important. Addictions, along with hope, belief, and faith, may show some outward effects in our lives; however, they are mental and inward attributes. The enemy uses addictions to keep us. The enemy will tell you not to seek help, not to attend meetings, not to go to church, not to contact your sponsor, pastor, or brother/sister in Christ because you are just going to do it again and we believe that liar. I promise you, if you hear others who went before you, you will see that you are not the only person who said, "I'm never doing that again" and did.

**The enemy uses addictions to keep us.**

---

[17] John 20:29

I can recall nights when I got so intoxicated, I swore with everything in me I wasn't going to drink again. Do you know what I did just a few days or a week later? Yep, you guessed it! I got even drunker the next time! But can I tell you I have been clean and sober for five years and counting now!

Hope. If it was possible for me, I promise you; it is possible for you! Don't let Satan, addictions, guilt, regret, embarrassment, shame, or whatever you are feeling stop you from obtaining your complete spiritual healing. You have to work the steps, and they are not a one-step stop. You have to keep working the steps, keep attending meetings, keep going to church, and stay connected because after all, *"faith comes by hearing and hearing by the Word of God."*[18] The more and more you do something and hear something, especially positive and hopeful things, the more and more you become what you are feeding yourself.

> Don't let Satan, addictions, guilt, regret, embarrassment, shame, or whatever you are feeling stop you from obtaining your complete spiritual healing.

---

[18] Romans 10:17

When it comes to hope, you have to cherish that desire of complete spiritual health and know that you can receive it. Once you receive complete spiritual health, don't allow anyone to take that away from you. Hold fast with a firm conviction, accepting that it is true, honest, genuine, and real. Know in your Know-Know (deep inside) that no matter how far away it may seem, firmly believe that there is hope for you and completely trust it, which brings us to Step 3: Trust in God.

*"Don't wait for tomorrow. Today, there is hope."*
*- Anonymous*

## Chapter 3:
## Trust in God

## Trust in God: "Decide to turn your will and your life over to the care of God the Eternal Father and His Son, Jesus Christ."[4]

*"Therefore humble yourselves under the mighty hand of God, that He may exalt you in due time, casting all your care upon Him, for He cares for you." - 1 Peter 5:6-7*

The third step in recovery is to trust in God. This step, to me, is an important step. Not that the other two steps we took thus far are not, but this step, is the step that we consciously take. In this step, we have a decision to make. We have to decide to turn our will and our life over to the care of God, Jesus, and the Holy Spirit. When we decide to take step number three and trust in God, we allow God to take over our unmanageable life (step one) and believe that His power can restore us (step two).

> *Jesus has to literally take the wheel; which means you have to let the wheel, your will, go.*

Addictions, however, can make taking this step hard. When we are caught up in our addictions and our sin, however deep we may be, it makes it hard to see the light. All we see are our addictions, our faults, our sins, our failures, our shortcomings, and what we keep doing even though we may no longer desire to do so. How can you trust in God when you can't even see yourself getting out of your mess? Once we take the first two steps, it makes it a little bit easier to take this one. Note: It is very important not to skip steps or do them out of order because each step you take prepares you for the steps to come. Honesty and hope (step one and two) allow us to at least play with the thought of giving God a chance, and eventually, we will.

> ***How can you trust in God when you can't even see yourself getting out of your mess?***

Remember how I shared with you earlier that I lost hope in becoming a wife and how God stepped in? Well, that is because I worked the steps and I exercised step three and trusted in Him. I made a conscious decision to turn my will and my life over to the care of God and Jesus and allowed the Holy Spirit to have His way. I made the decision that I was going to give God full reign over my life and my relationships. I humbled myself under His mighty hand, cast my cares upon Him, and in due time, He exalted me.

Was it easy? Heck no! Were there times where I fell even after making that decision? Yes, I did. However, I kept working the steps. I didn't let my failings or Satan keep me from continuing on my journey. I kept attending meetings. I kept going to church and Bible study. I kept being honest. I remained hopeful, believing it was possible for me. I kept the faith, and I kept trusting in God. I knew that I could not do it on my own; there was no more leaning to my own understanding, and from that moment on, I knew nothing but trusting in God.

Proverbs 3: 7-8 says, *"Do not be wise in your own eyes; Fear the Lord and depart from evil. It will be health to your flesh, and strength to your bones."* Let me repeat, "health to your flesh and strength to your bones." Are your addictions healthy to your flesh and strengthening your bones? I have seen firsthand how addictions, drugs, alcohol, sex, and money can weaken both your flesh and your bones. These things will lead you to do something strange for some change. Your addictions make you someone you're not; they make you do things you wouldn't normally do. But can I tell you that you are not your sins and that your addictions are not you! Hallelujah!

Chapter 7 in the book of Romans talks about the war between the flesh and spirit. This is a serious war that we (addicts, believers, saved and unsaved alike) fight every day. When you make the conscious decision to trust in God and to surrender and give your life to Christ, all hell breaks loose!

Temptation appears, and your addictions get stronger. Why? All because Satan does not want you clean. He does not want you on the winning team. Satan wants to keep you bound to your addictions, he wants to keep you in your sin, and he wants your life to be hopeless and unmanageable. However, Jesus does not want that life for you; He desires something much better. Jesus says it like this in John 10:10,

> **You are not your sins. Your addictions are not you.**

"*The thief* (Satan) *does not come except to steal, and to kill, and to destroy. I* (Jesus) *have come that they* (you and I) *may have life, and that they* (you and I) *may have it* (life) ***MORE abundantly.***"

*Don't you want an abundant life?*

## ONE STEP AT A TIME: TRUST IN GOD

When we decide to trust God and turn our will and our lives over to Him and invite Him into our hearts, we give up the power of the flesh and are now under the power of the Spirit. Therefore, we walk after the Spirit and not after the flesh. Good news, right!

The Bible tells us in Galatians 5:16 that if we walk in the Spirit and not in the flesh, we will not fulfill the lusts of the flesh. In other words, that last drink, that last hit, that last rendezvous was your "one more (fill in the blank)." Walking in the Spirit, with the Spirit, and after the Spirit is what will keep us from giving in to our addictions time and time again.

This step is probably the easiest yet most complicated step that we can take. Easy because we don't have to do anything but let go and trust in God; hard because

**God is right there too. Even when He seems like He's not; He is.**

we actually have let go and trust in God. Jesus has to literally take the wheel; which means you have to let the wheel, *your will*, go. When you are used to something being a certain way, it can be hard to make a change or accept change. Depending on how far or how deep you are in your addictions and sin, change can seem impossible. After we become honest (step one) and obtain hope (step two), we come to know that change is possible; therefore, we can let go and trust in God (step three).

> There is nothing good that dwells in our flesh (Romans 7:18a), and if we continue to trust in ourselves, we will continue to fail. God is the One who can help us. However, the question is, do you want His help? Will you trust Him?

As stated in meetings, the steps only work if you work them. This is a step I think will have to be worked a little more than the others. In the midst of trusting God, it can sometimes seem that He is not there. When our itch, that urge or craving begins, and our sin and addictions are naturally present, it's easier to give in.

*I mean it's right there, so why not?!* But do you know that God is right there too? Even when He seems like He's not; He is. Deuteronomy 31:6 says it like this: *"Be strong and of good courage, do not fear nor be afraid of them; for the Lord your God, He is the One who goes with you. He will not leave you nor forsake you."* You don't have to give into that addiction or that temptation. Fight the urge, be strong and be courageous. You cannot do it on your own, and the great news is, you don't have to because He is right there with you.

Along with trusting God, you have to have patience. Just like trust in a natural relationship is built, your trust in God has to be built up as well. No, your addictions will not go away the moment you realize you have them, so you have to continue to make the conscious decision over and over to trust in God and to give your will over to Him because I guarantee, if you trust in yourself and think you can do it on your own, you will fail! Every time!

However, there is a condition that comes with trusting in God. You have to do so with all your heart: not some, but all. We are given this instruction in the third chapter of the book of Proverbs, verses five. To overcome your addictions, you have to trust in the Lord with ALL your heart and lean not on your own understanding. Remember that God is in control, so it only makes sense to trust Him, right? When our addictions were stronger than us, we trusted our addictions, but now we know that God is stronger than us AND our addictions – we can trust in Him.

Since trust is built, I must tell you that there may be times when you fail, but do not fret.

It is in those times that the steps are most important. You cannot give up. You have to continue working the steps. You have to trust God when He says to cast your cares upon Him because He cares for you. You have to trust God when He says He has chosen you and has not cast you away. You have to trust God when He says He is with you always. You have to trust God when He says to trust Him and, in all ways, acknowledge Him and He will direct your paths. You have to trust God when He says your past is your past and in Him, old things have passed away, and all things are made new.[19]

There is a song by an artist named Lauren Daigle called *Trust in You* that I believe illustrates the steps at work in the midst of the song. When you get a chance, take a listen.

In the meantime, don't allow Satan to get into your head and make you lose hope and stop trusting. Remember, he is out to steal, kill, and destroy you! You better recognize the devil knows just what you like, you have not been saved and clean all your life!

> **The devil knows just what you like, you better recognize! You haven't been saved and clean all your life!**

---

[19] 1 Peter 5:7, Isaiah 41:9b, Matthew 28:20b, Proverbs 3:5-6, 2 Corinthians 5:17

But you can be for the rest of your life. That is the good news. When our addictions come up, and we continue to work step three, we will begin to see ourselves in a new light with a newfound life, and this leads us to our next step: Truth.

*"If only people worked God like they worked their addictions."*
-*Anonymous*

## Chapter 4:
*Truth*

## Truth: "Make a searching and fearless written moral inventory of yourself."[4]

*"Examine yourselves as to whether you are in the faith. Test yourselves. Do you not know yourselves, that Jesus Christ is in you? —unless indeed you are disqualified. But I trust that you will know that we are not disqualified."*
- 2 Corinthians 13:5-6

The fourth step in recovery is truth. In this step, we are to make a written moral inventory of ourselves. This written moral inventory is called a "Life Story." When you write your life story, you are documenting all the events that took place in your life: good, bad, and ugly. It is only natural that this step is next. We already came to terms that we cannot manage our own lives and that only God can heal us completely, and we made the conscious decision to trust God, so writing a moral inventory, or life story, of ourselves, should be easy, so you think. Because we are creatures, who like to justify things, being 100 percent truthful may not be that easy. This is why we need the Holy Spirit.

*It's true or it's false.*

## One Step at a Time: Truth

In this step, you have to search for the inventory, which means you have to dig and dive deep within yourselves and you have to do it fearlessly, so you cannot let your fears stop you from seeing the true you. The truth will not always be pretty and to be honest, we will probably like it more if we can skip this step, but this step is much needed and very important in the recovery process. In order to obtain true healing and salvation, we have to be honest with ourselves. In the words of my Elect Lady Wency Casby, "If you want to be healed, you got to be real." In this stage, we cannot justify. Everything has to be black and white. It's true or it's false. This is the only way to true recovery.

In step one, we only admitted that we are powerless over our sins and addictions and they caused our lives to become unmanageable. Step 1 was realizing, *"I have a problem. I am a sinner in need of a Savior."* Step four, on the other hand, makes us dive deep into our lives to prepare us for the steps ahead. This step will bring up events and resentments that we may have buried in the back of our minds from which we need healing and deliverance. So, although this may seem like a repeated step, it's not.

Remember in the chapter on Hope; I told you how I began to lose hope that I would be a wife? Truth is, if I would have kept giving into my flesh and continued with my addiction, I would have never become one. My lifestyle was telling me that I will always be an appetizer and never an entrée and that was presently true. My truth was not pretty, but my truth also didn't line up with the way I was feeling.

> **Just as the steps are instructions and a way of life to the addict; the Word of God is the same to believers.**

### *You are an addict, but you are not your addictions*

We can even look at God's truth, which is His Word (The Holy Bible). Just as the steps are instructions and a way of life to the addict; the Word of God is the same to believers.

*"All Scripture is given by inspiration of God, and is profitable for doctrine, for reproof, for correction, for*

*instruction in righteousness, that the man of God may be complete, thoroughly equipped for every good work."*[20]

God's Word gives us the tools to live a life of recovery as the new creation we are. Not only that, but it is a great weapon of spiritual warfare. Just take a look at how Jesus combated Satan when he was trying to tempt Jesus in the wilderness in Matthew 4. Every time Satan came at Jesus trying to tempt Jesus, Jesus' responses started with "*It is written:*"

Satan: "*If You are the Son of God, command that these stones become bread.*"

Jesus: "***It is written****, 'Man should not live by bread alone, but by every word that proceeds from the mouth of God.'*"

Satan: "*If You are the Son of God, throw Yourself down. For it is written: 'He shall give His angels charge over you' and 'in their hands they shall bear you up, lest you dash your foot against a stone.'*"

---

[20] 2 Timothy 3:16-17

Jesus: "***It is written*** *again, 'You shall not tempt the Lord your God.'*"

Satan: "*All these things I will give You if You will fall down and worship me.*"

Jesus: "*Away with you Satan! For **it is written**, 'You shall worship the Lord your God, and Him only you shall serve.'*"[21]

Satan even tried to use the scripture against Jesus. This tells me that Satan will try to use you against you. What I mean is, Satan will attempt to get you to fall back into sin and addiction by using a tactic that you are very familiar with; however, in my sanctified imagination, before Jesus answered, He examined Himself. Hence the word "again" in His second reply.

Jesus knew the Word. He knew His truth because that's who He is (Reference John 1:1 and John 14:6) and we also need to know our truth and who God says we are to combat Satan and his tactics! Therefore, as we make this moral

---

[21] Matthew 4:1-11

inventory (examining ourselves), and we write down how we were and the things we have done or been through; we can utilize the Word of God – God's truth – to say, "Although I have written my life story, it is written again." "*But as for you, you meant evil against me; but God meant it for good.*"[22]

It is a good thing that God knows and searches the heart. Nine out of ten addicts do not want to be addicts. You are an addict, but you are not your addictions. There's the difference. While in active addiction, the time

**You are a child of God and you are forgiven.**

where I was actively drinking and committing adultery, I was the side-chick, however, that was not my true self. When I made a searching and fearless, written moral inventory of myself, I realized that I was so much more. I realized that I was a wife and not just a side-chick. To make it even better, God told me that my sins were forgiven, and my slate was made clean when Jesus died on the cross, and His blood was shed for me. My dear sister, my dear brother, right now, you may be a drunk, junkie, adulterer, or

---

[22] Genesis 50:20

whatever, but know that beyond that, you are so much more. You are a child of God and you are forgiven.

As humans, we tend to believe what people say about us. Sometimes it may be true, but I find most times it is not always true. However, when God shows you who you are, you can bet your last dollar (unless gambling is your addiction) that it is truth. After all, He is the One who created you and me.

When we operate in truth and make a moral inventory of ourselves, it will be our truth. We cannot argue with the Bible when it says, "*every man is right in his own eyes.*"[23] So, because of this, you have to wonder, "*How truthful will my inventory be?*" Therefore, when working this step, I believe that we are to write our own truth but with God's help.

> **I am an overcomer!**

If you ask an addict about the steps, they will tell you that step four is the hardest for them. The reason why this step is so hard and not always pretty is because you have to revisit some places, thoughts, emotions, situations, and possibly even events that you want to forget, but there is beauty in this. The truth will not always be pretty, that is

---

[23] Proverbs 21:2a

why you cannot let your fears stop you from being real with yourself. The more you are truthful with yourself, the freer you are from what's holding you.

> *Challenge:*
> *Write down your truth about what you think and say about yourself and then write down God's truth of what He thinks and says about you.*

Listen to me; the steps are not going to get easier. Each minute we are out of our addiction is a minute we overcame. That is truth. Write that down, "I am an overcomer." You got one piece of self-inventory down. Way to go you! However, it does not stop there.

One person we can ask about being truthful is our dear friend Leah. From the Bible, we know that Leah was the older sister of Rachel and her *"eyes were delicate,"* or weak. Rachel, on the other hand, was *"beautiful of form and appearance."*[24] As if that wasn't enough truth, Jacob loved Rachel, the younger sister, enough to work for her for seven

---

[24] Genesis 29:17

years, but when he completed his seven years, he thought he was getting Rachel, the one he worked for. However, Laban, their father, gave Jacob Leah instead. Poor thing.

When Jacob realized that he was bamboozled, the next morning after marrying and sleeping with her, he was highly upset! Laban then insisted that Jacob be with her for a week, then he can have the one he wanted, Rachel. Not only was Leah the one not chosen, but she was given to a man in secret; then to make matters worse, he only stayed with her and dealt with her because he was promised the younger sister. Talk about an ugly truth.

> **Your truth is what will bring a praise out of you.**

But here's the thing, Leah's truth seems ugly on the surface, but just wait and see, it's really beautiful underneath.

Things began to look up for Leah. *"When the Lord saw that Leah was unloved, He opened her womb,"*[25] and she started to bear children. Ironically enough, Leah wasn't working the steps though. Not just yet. You see, Leah's addiction was love. She wanted to be loved and wanted so badly to be loved by Jacob, that she had children and named them in hopes for her husband to *"love her"* and *"become*

---

[25] Genesis 29:31a

*attached to her because she has borne him three sons."*[26] Sounds familiar?

It wasn't until the fourth child that Leah made a searching and fearless, moral written inventory of herself. Leah named her fourth child, Judah, which means "Praise." Leah realized that having children for Jacob was not going to get him to love her; therefore, she was honest with herself, obtained hope, trusted in God, and became truthful with and of herself and gave God some praise for it! Leah got her act together after four children. Get it? Four steps, four children. We can look at it as if every child was a step for Leah.

I pray that having multiple children will not have to be the answer for you to be truthful with yourself. From this story, you realize that no matter what pain, rejection, or defeat you had to endure, you can be truthful with yourself and your truth will cause you to praise.

### *How truthful will your inventory be?*

I can only imagine what it was like for Leah to see Jacob with Rachel, knowing that she had children for him, but he

---

[26] Genesis 29:32b, 29:34

didn't love her; or at least in the way that he loved Rachel. That had to be devastating. Ignorant to me, I do not know how many years apart the boys were, but I bet that trip down memory lane, from one to four, to get that inventory down was not so beautiful for Leah. But she did it and so can you!

So, can we be honest? Can we search fearlessly and write an inventory of ourselves? How does your list look? Remember, your truth may not be as pretty or even as ugly as the next one, but it is your truth, and yes, you have to accept it. After all, the truth shall set you free, which brings us to our next step: Confession.

*"I got a second chance to make a first impression."* -Anonymous

## Chapter 5:
### Confession

## One Step at a Time: Confession

**Confession: "Admit to yourself, to your Heavenly Father in the name of Jesus Christ, to proper priesthood authority, and to another person the exact nature of your wrongs."[4]**

*"He who covers his sins will not prosper, but whoever confesses and forsakes them will have mercy."*
*- Proverbs 28:13*

The fifth step in recovery is confession. Here, we are told to admit to ourselves and to God, in Jesus' name (important thing), to proper priesthood authority (pastors and the like), and to another person the exact nature of your wrongs (that other person could very well be the person that you have wronged or just a trusted friend). It is no mistake that this is the next step. We just finished writing an inventory of ourselves, and I am pretty sure some bad, rude, conniving, deceitful, and ugly things came up that we need to confess.

*Isolation is never the answer.*

On the flip side, confession may not be the next thing on your mind that you want to do. Being as we just finished a written inventory of ourselves, we may have the feeling to distance ourselves from others because of the shame and embarrassment, but that is not what will help you on the road to recovery. Isolation is never the answer.

Confession, to me, is a step of relief. It comes right after we realize that we did some stuff and now talking about it and admitting it will make us feel better. Confession, just like the prior steps, may not be that easy to do. It may be hard to actually voice all of your wrongs, but the Bible says: *"he who covers his sins will not prosper, but whoever confesses and forsakes them will have mercy."*[27] Mercy is something we all need!

Confession is important because when you cover your sins, you will not prosper, meaning you will still be in your mess and not on the road to recovery. When you cannot voice your wrongdoings, you are still being held by them. I know firsthand how hard it may be to confess some things because when you are under the influence, there are some things you may do that you wouldn't normally do if you were in your right mind. Because of this, you are not going to want to admit that, which means you won't confess it,

---

[27] Proverbs 28:13

but a good indication that you are totally free from your addiction is when you can tell others about it.

However, if we are to go in the order that the action steps tell us to go in, then the action step of confession should be worded as follows: "Admit to your Heavenly Father in the name of Jesus Christ, to yourself, to proper priesthood authority, and to another person the exact nature of your wrongs." God should be the first one we confess to.

When it comes to confessing your wrongs to God, it shouldn't be hard, but often it is. You see, God knows all you have done. Everything right and wrong under the sun. One would think that this should make it easier because He already knows, but to get yourself to say it and hear it come out of your own mouth is not so pleasant. However, when we confess and admit the nature of our wrongdoings to God, we are rewarded with a forgiveness that surpasses them all and a super clean slate. What's even more rewarding, is the forgiveness you receive and the relief that you feel afterward. Not only that, but He will give us the grace and

> **A good indication that you are totally free from your addiction, is when you can tell others about it.**

confidence we need to confess to others, especially ourselves.

Therefore, the next confession should be to you. This confession is the next hardest one to do. To tell yourself how you played yourself like a fool and did some ungodly, lowdown and dirty things, all for what!? A few minutes of pleasure!? That is not going to make you feel good at all. But it is necessary. It is part of the steps. We can sometimes be our biggest critics and hard on ourselves, even harder than God is on us, but this part is essential. We will get to that later.

In the midst of confession, especially to yourself, you may run into some complications. These complications arise when you let Satan play with your mind and take your voice. Since Satan wants to keep us in bondage to our sin and addictions, he tries to make us feel bad about letting others know about what we have done wrong, but you cannot allow or afford to let the enemy win! Satan has taken so much of our lives already that we owe it to ourselves to recover. Don't let Satan take your voice too.

> **Don't let Satan take your voice too.**

When I made it to step number five, I was pretty much over the recovery process. After doing a full inventory of myself, I saw myself for who I really was, and she was not pretty at all. Then I was told I have to confess my wrongs. To who?! WHAT!? Me?? No, I think I'll just confess and ask God for forgiveness and move on.

As I attempted to move on, I was still living in fear. Living with the fear that I may fail again, and it seemed as if even though I moved on, I was still in my addictions and in my sin. My life was becoming unmanageable, and we already stated how an unmanageable life is not life.

Eventually, I came to terms that this was part of recovery for a reason and I had a sit down with myself. I laid out every dirty little secret I had, the sins I tried to cover with denial and justification (because we are too good at that, right?) and put it all out on the table. Was it fun and pretty? Not at all! There were a lot of tears shed and a whole bunch of reality checks, but the end result was very pleasant. I felt lighter, freer, and inspired to continue with my journey.

Confession is like forgiveness. It is not for the other person as much as it is for you and had I not completed this process; I would not be sitting here writing this book and telling you that it is possible for you too! I could have attempted to continue working the steps, but it would not have worked because the steps are designed to work in order. The steps before always prepare you for the steps ahead, and they encompass the foundation of what you need to go through to work them. If I would not have completed this step, I would have still been stuck here on this level.

## *When you don't confess or can't confess, truth is, you may still be in your mess...*

You've heard the saying, "Confession is good for the soul," and it is. When you don't confess or can't confess, truth is, you may still be in your mess, and if you are still in your mess, your faults, your wrongdoings, your addictions, and your sin can and will blackmail you! When your addictions and your sins blackmail you, they hold your life for ransom. You may be able to move on and may even be clean and sober for a while, but deep down inside, you'll know and feel that something is holding you back.

> **Accountability is something you need on this journey.**

Something is. That "something" could be embarrassment, shame, guilt, or even regret, but you have to let those things go, and you do that by speaking it! Once you get the confession between you and God and you and yourself out of the way, confessing to the proper priesthood and another person should be smooth sailing! It is important for you to find the right church home. It is essential to confession and recovery.

As stated before, church should be like a meeting place for addicts. In Jeremiah 3:15, God shares how He will give us shepherds after His heart who will feed us with knowledge and understanding. So, if the shepherd (proper priesthood) has a heart according to God's heart, confessing to them should feel like confessing to God all over again.

Not to mention, God possibly already gave your proper priesthood insight on you. If so, your confessions can turn into confirmations. In return, those confirmations will increase your hope and make you trust God even more as you continue on the road to recovery!

> *You have to keep things in the light so that Satan cannot use them against you in the dark*

Lastly, this step says to confess to another person the exact nature of your faults. This part of the step can be a little bit tricky. Who can you trust? In meetings, you are encouraged to get a sponsor, and that is what this part is suggesting. I believe this part is equally as important as the others. Confessing your faults to another person, whom you trust, will help keep you on track. How do you ask? I will tell you.

Typically, the person you choose to confess to will be someone close to you and someone who has a similar background as you. This means that the person knows you and knows what you are going through and if they been through it themselves, they will have insight to help you get through. All of this will help them keep you accountable, and accountability on this journey is something you need.

There is one last thing you need to know about confession. Confession is an ongoing process; it is not a one-stop shop. You have to keep things in the light so that Satan cannot use them against you in the dark.

*"For everyone practicing evil hates the light and does not come to the light, lest his deeds should be exposed. But he who does the truth comes to the light, that his deeds may be clearly seen, that they have been done in God"* [28]

If you are living a life of recovery, following Jesus, it shouldn't be a problem to keep things in the light. There

---

[28] John 3:20-21

should be nothing to hide unless you are practicing evil (alcoholic hanging in the bars, single in Christ sleeping with your boy/girlfriend), and as long as you are in the light, others can see your good deeds.

> *Challenge:*
> *If you haven't confessed your faults to God and yourself as of yet, please do so. Then identify your proper priesthood and another person(s) you can trust and have a confession session with each of them, confessing the exact nature of your wrongdoings.*

Remember, confession is good for the soul. So, get out of yourself enough to confess your wrongdoings because the show must still go on. Now, let's move on to a change of heart.

*"You can't be forgiven and granted a clean slate unless you confess that you are wrong."* - *Anonymous*

## Chapter 6:
## Change of Heart

## Change of Heart: "Become entirely ready to have God remove all your character weaknesses."[4]

*"Create in me a clean heart, O God, and renew a steadfast spirit within me." - Psalm 51:10*

So here we are. Congratulations! You got your life together; you got some hope, you are walking in it and trusting God. You know who you are, and you shared your wrongs with others, but something is wrong. That "itch" is still there, isn't it?

It is highly possible as you continue to journey along the road of recovery that you will be tempted by the very thing you are in recovery for. You may even feel confused and weak because it just seems as if you cannot shake it. I have some great news for you though: YOU CAN!

I can recall chilling with a guy one night during my single season in the late hours of the night. Now, I knew our "relationship" wasn't going anywhere; however, I was still okay with hanging out with him during the late hours of the night. (Red flag!)

Anyway, I made up my mind that we were not going to have sex. I was okay with kissing, but that was as far as it was going. Well, for the sake of text, it was about to go down! However, one of my favorite verses resonated in that very moment: *"No temptation has overtaken you except such as is common to man; but God is faithful, who will not allow you to be tempted beyond what you are able, but with the temptation will also make the way of escape, that you may be able to bear it."*[29]

God indeed showed Himself faithful and made a way of escape. That night showed me that although I may have had my mind made up, it was my heart that needed changing.

> It is highly possible as you continue to journey along the road of recover that you are still tempted by the very thing you are in recovery for.

This chapter focuses on the heart because it is a heart condition and if your heart isn't right, it can stop you dead in your tracks on the road to recovery. As you become clean and sober and come out of sin and darkness, you will have to adjust to the way things are "now." At the beginning of my journey to recovery, I had to learn how to cope without drinking and having sex. At first, it was easy because no temptation or stimulating situation was occurring, and this

---

[29] 1 Corinthians 10:13

went on for a few months until what happened to my grandfather.

One night, I went out with a friend to support another friend, and I got a call that my grandfather had a heart attack. After that night, he was doing well, but about a few weeks later, I was at a water park and came back to a phone full of messages and voicemails! I had no idea what was going on, but I knew it wasn't good. My grandfather was in the hospital unresponsive.

For the most part, I was able to pull it together. I was working the steps, remaining prayerful, and keeping the faith until six weeks later – my grandfather passed away. I was in shock and denial in the beginning, but then the temptations started to kick in. I was trying my best to keep on track, but since the devil knew me longer than I have been saved, clean, and sober, he knew exactly what I wanted (notice I didn't say "needed"). I would pass by the daiquiri shop, and my mouth would salivate. I would see a bottle of wine and the smell would entice me.

I would remember all the "fun" I had and how I had no care in the world when I was intoxicated. I would open and lock my phone so many times as I contemplated on sending that message or making that phone call. I was empty. I was hurt. I was weak. There was nothing I could do, and all the steps, Bible verses and things I've heard at church didn't seem helpful. I wondered, *Why should I even bother when God let my grandfather die!* I thought, *I need to drink until I forget how I feel and then give myself away because I don't even want to be bothered with myself.*

But remember how the steps only work if you work them? Well, in the midst of all of the back and forth that was going on in my mind; I kept attending meetings (going to church), and I remember sitting there, still trying to figure out why I'm still there, and hearing the Pastor say things like (and I am paraphrasing):

"Be God-conscious and not sin conscious, whatever you think on, you'll attract."

"Living right don't exempt you from trouble; it helps get you through trouble."

"Be honest with yourself. Know your weakness and your strengths."

"The devil will always try to get you at your most vulnerable moment and will try to come in and capture you in your mind, that's why you have to take your thoughts captive."

"He/she who controls your mind controls your destiny."

Eventually, I realized that I was worrying and focusing on the wrong things and I had to get myself together! I revisited the previous steps and came to have a change of heart.

**_Better recognize, the devil knows just what you like. You haven't been saved, clean and sober all your life._**

You see, before Christ and before this road to recovery, my way of coping was alcohol. I wasn't far into my recovery or strong enough in my faith when my grandpa died to react differently. Initially, I wanted to drink to cope with the pain and the hurt I was dealing with; but do you know that God is near the brokenhearted?[30]

God reminded me of Isaiah 55:8 where it says, "*For My thoughts are not your thoughts, Nor are your ways My ways,*" and I had to shift my focus and change my mindset. I needed to remember Philippians 4:8, "*Finally, brethren, whatever things are true, whatever things are noble, whatever things are just, whatever things are pure, whatever things are lovely, whatever things are of good report, if*

---

[30] Psalm 34:18

*there is any virtue and if there is anything praiseworthy— meditate on these things."* I also needed to *"bring every thought into captivity to the obedience of Christ"* like 2 Corinthians 10:5 says.

By doing so, I was able to better cope and receive my healing from my grandfather's passing. I thought that I was in the safe zone because I was doing so well before his death, but then I found myself powerless and in an unmanageable place.

I don't want you to make the same mistake I did and think that since you made it through the previous steps, that the rest of the road to recovery would be easy given the fact that the first five steps were kind of challenging because they are not. In fact, Step 6 is normally where you begin to find some turns and forks in the road.

> We need a change of heart so we can have a chance at living.

### *God is near the brokenhearted*

In step six, you can feel empty and weak, so this is why you have to become entirely ready to have God remove all of your character weaknesses. If you want to continue on this journey, you have to be strengthened, and you must have your strength in the Lord. You must have a change of heart and allow God to do a work in you. Again, you will need to give up your self-control and allow God to have His way with and in you. This is important because God's strength is made perfect in our weakness,[31] in other words, where we are weak, He is strong.

When you come out of your sin and your addictions, you begin to see things a little different. You begin to feel different, and slowly but surely, things and people will begin to slip away. You will no longer have the same access to or the desire for your old addictions. You will even lose relationships with some people who used to share your addictions, and this can become a bit lonely. This loneliness can have you feeling vulnerable, and since the devil knows your triggers, he will start to try and use your feelings against you. But why the heart?

The heart is a very vital organ. Without the heart pumping blood throughout our bodies, we would not be able to survive – we would die. Furthermore, if the heart is sick or damaged, it can affect the entire body. This is why I believe Jesus enters into our hearts – to change our hearts. It

---

[31] 2 Corinthians 12:9

plays such a vital role in our physical lives, so, to me, it only makes sense for it to play a vital role in our spiritual lives.

We need a change of heart so that we can have a chance at living. However, you cannot change your heart on your own; you need God. Had God not changed my heart when my grandfather passed away, I would have surely started using/abusing alcohol again. Drinking was pretty much my character. "Today was a good day, let's drink." "Today was bad day, let's drink." "Today was just a day, let's drink to that anyway!" I was pretty strong when I started this journey of recovery, but then life happened, and I realized I was still weak. However, my relapse/backsliding prevention plan started to form on the day that I started this road to recovery.

***This is what I want you to know, dear reader. Life is going to happen. It does not, and it will not stop when you decide to get your life right. But recovery is worth it!***

Earlier, I mentioned how God is strong when we are weak, which is why we need to rely on Him and become entirely ready for Him to remove all of our character weaknesses. Character. Weakness. So why not just weaknesses?

**I googled the word "character," and this is the first definition to pop up:**

1. The mental and moral qualities distinctive to an individual:
 a. The distinctive nature of something
 b. The quality of being individual, typically in an interesting or unusual way
 c. Strength and originality in a person's nature
 d. A person's good reputation
 e. A written statement of someone's good qualities; a recommendation

*And He said to me, "My grace is sufficient for you, for My strength is made perfect in weakness."*[32]

Character is the very essence of who we are. If there is weakness in our character, there is weakness in us. This step

---

[32] 2 Corinthians 12:9a

tells us to be *entirely ready* for God to remove all of our character weaknesses. We must be ready because the change will be something new and it must become something that you get used to. For example:

If you have been eating meat all or even the majority of your life and then decide to become a vegetarian, do you think that will come easy for you? I doubt it. It may go well for a few days, maybe even a week or two, but by the time the end of the month or so rolls around, your stomach is going to speak out and say, "FEED ME MEAT!" Are you going to do it? Without the full information, probably.

Before deciding to become a vegetarian, you received some news from the doctor. The doctor told you that if you stop eating meat, you will become healthier, happier, and experience life in a whole new light. However, if you continue to eat meat, your life may seem to be going well, but in reality, you are causing the quality of your life to deteriorate. Now, what are you going to do?

From that story, the "meat" represents our addictions and our sin which are causing us damnation, and God, being the "doctor," is trying to help us live a more abundant life. So, He gives us instructions to follow ("stop eating meat, and you will become healthier, happier, and experience life in a whole new light"). Our "stomachs," or our minds, will tell us to continue indulging because they have become accustomed to the toxic things (sins and addictions).

Because of this, we need a change of heart and having that change of heart will make it easier to make the conscious decision, day after day, and sometimes, moment by moment to do the right thing.

Just like the previous steps, it may not be a fun one to follow or even an easy one, but it is necessary for recovery. This step is essential to the journey, and as I've mentioned before, the steps are made to work in order, so we cannot skip this step no matter how hard it may be.

How do I know this? Because this was the hardest chapter for me to write, but it was necessary, and now that it is completed, I can move on and so can you. This step is to prepare you for the remainder of your journey. The steps that come next require a change in character, a change of heart, and now you have that. This change should make you humble.

*"You have a desire, but can you commit to the desire?"* -*Anonymous*

# Chapter 7:
## Humility

## Humility: "Humbly ask the Heavenly Father to remove your shortcomings."[4]

*"Humble yourselves in the sight of the Lord, and He will lift you up."* - James 4:10

Are you kidding me?! First, you tell me I was weak; now you tell me I have shortcomings. Great!

Calm down, calm down. This is not a bad thing. Once you saw your weaknesses, you should have seen your shortcomings.

It only makes sense why this step is next. Sometimes in recovery, you fall, and that's okay because you have God's mercy to help you along the way. However, you must have the right heart. You need a remorseful heart. Being as we just had a change of heart, this step should be easy, but that is not always the case.

When I was drinking, I felt invincible. I was confident, bold, and cocky. Sounds familiar? Yep. Liquid courage. In those moments, I did what I wanted to do when I wanted to do it, and not think twice about it. Actually, I was pretty ashamed of some of the stuff that I've done. Luckily, I had Steps 1-6 to get me here.

Steps 1-6 showed me how "weak" I was and how low I have become. By the time I made it to Step 7, I found myself needing to be humbled. I was at a place where it was just me. Well, just me and God. At the beginning of my recovery, I was alone a lot of times. This was not because I was choosing to be isolated from others; it was just that my circle changed as my life changed. Honestly, in return, that isolation led me closer to Christ to be able to humbly ask Him to remove my shortcomings.

In the beginning, due to the isolation, it wasn't hard to talk to and with God and to ask for His help to remove my shortcomings, because I wanted to be better. However, as I continued to grow, this step became a bit more challenging. What do I mean? Let me tell you.

> Sometimes in recovery, you fall, and that's okay, because you have God's mercy to help you along the way.

Prior to marriage, I prepared for marriage. I would do things as if I were already married. I watched my spending, learned how to cook new and different meals, etc. It was fun, it was therapeutic, and it was easy! But the key point, I was still single. Well, let's fast-forward to marriage. I have to ask God to humble me constantly. With this new role of being a wife, working, (I was not working before marriage), and readjusting, I realized how short I was coming up in my marriage. It was easier when I was single because I didn't have the outside stimuli of actually having a husband; however, after I got married, I had to live out the very thing I was preparing for; I had to revisit this step.

> ***Shortcomings are not bad. Shortcomings are simply flaws, and we all have them.***

God will continue to show you yourself and your shortcomings on the road to recovery, and it is up to you if you will ask and allow Him to help you. Let me tell you though; it will not be easy. You see, I like doing things when I want to do them. However, that is not the case when you are married. Look, I would like to tell you that I am that perfect, Biblical wife, but then I would be lying. Each day, I do a moral inventory where I see all of my shortcomings – DAILY – and I have to humbly ask the Heavenly Father to remove them.

Shortcomings are not bad. Shortcomings are simply flaws, and we all have them, so there is no need for you to feel like this step is extra. We need the strength of the Holy Spirit to make it through this journey. Some of our flaws are small, and some are big, but regardless of the size, we have them.

When we are in addiction, we don't realize our flaws because it may be normal to us, but when we line them up against the Word of God, we see that they are not normal. Not only are they not normal, but they're wrong.

One shortcoming I had in my addiction was lying. I just had to lie, and sometimes there was no reason to lie. When I wasn't lying for fun, I was lying to be sneaky. Well, eventually, all the lies caught up with me. My mom could have been a PI (Private Investigator). She caught me in so many lies, whether it was her great PI skills or just my lack of skills, to where she just lost all trust in me.

> God wants our relationship with Him to be strong, but not only that, He wants us strong in our journey to recovery as well.

### *Have you ever lost trust in someone or have them lose trust in you?*

This was one of the hardest seasons I had to go through as an adolescent. When I did realize my shortcomings (lying) and changed my ways (started telling the truth), she still didn't fully believe me. I had to SHOW her better than I could tell her. By making that decision to change my ways, my relationship with my mother is now stronger than ever!

> *An "I got this" attitude takes God out of the equation. The minute you feel and believe that YOU got this, you are no longer walking/living in humility. You my friend are now in pride.*

That is the whole purpose of this step. God wants our relationship with Him to be strong, but not only that, He wants us strong in our journey to recovery as well, but we have a choice to make. We have to decide to humbly ask God to remove our shortcomings.

If we are to be honest, some of us don't mind our shortcoming or think that they are "big" enough to ask God to remove them, but that's what causes us to remain in addiction. Shortcomings are what keep us from being our whole self. Granted, we will never be perfect, but each day we should be striving for perfection, which is to be like Jesus Christ.

I mentioned earlier how, due to my isolation, it was easy for me to ask God to remove my shortcomings, but as I continued to grow, it became harder. Growing in my faith, growing on my journey, growing in my life and the changes that came with it made it harder to humbly ask God to remove my shortcomings. Why is that? I'm glad you asked! It became harder for me to do step 7 because I had the attitude of "I got this." Did you catch it?

***A prideful heart will not let you make it past step 7.***

I, me, Danika, got this. Did I really? No. If I did, I wouldn't be in recovery, now would I? Not at all. An "I got this" attitude takes God out of the equation, and when God is out of the equation, the problem will never be solved. The whole time when I was in my addiction, I thought I was in control. I thought that I could manage and salvage my own life. I thought that I controlled the alcohol and the sex and not the other way around. "I can stop drinking when I'm ready," "I can stop sleeping around until I'm in a 'meaningful relationship.'"

> **We need the strength of the Holy Spirit to make it through this journey.**

## ONE STEP AT A TIME: HUMILITY

These were the things that I would say and think to myself. Can I tell you that I fell short EVERY time! It wasn't until I started this journey of recovery and started working the steps that I realized I was not in control and that I could not do this on my own.

I indulged in self which made it harder for me to not only see my shortcomings, but it made it harder for me to go to God with humility and ask Him to remove them. By not acknowledging my shortcomings and asking God to remove them, I kept coming up short in a lot of areas in my life, even after working steps 1-6. This sometimes happens on this journey, and if we are not careful, it will lead us back into our addictions. Regardless of where you are in life, or how much you think you've mastered something, do not get to the point where you think you got it all together. You have to be careful that you don't get big headed in this walk, which is another part of recovery for a reason.

This step calls for humility for a reason. But let's be honest, who wants to be the bigger person in any situation? I can say most times, that person is not me, but we have to be the bigger person whether we want to or not. We HAVE to remain humble on this journey. The minute you feel and believe that YOU got this, you are no longer walking/living in humility. You, my friend, are now operating in pride and a prideful heart will not let you make it past step 7.

*"What you gonna do now? Because the same opportunity is gonna come again for you to do the same thing."* -Anonymous

# Chapter 8:
## Seeking Forgiveness

## Seeking Forgiveness: "Make a written list of all persons you have harmed and become willing to make restitution to them."4

*"Therefore, as the elect of God, holy and beloved, put on tender mercies, kindness, humility, meekness, longsuffering; bearing with one another, and forgiving one another, if anyone has a complaint against another; even as Christ forgave you, so you also must do." - Colossians 3:12-13*

Welcome to Step 8! I pray that humility has rolled over and is still being exercised because you are going to need it still. I was torn between two verses when it came to this chapter, but I was led to believe this one is the best to fit. Here, on step 8, we are seeking forgiveness by writing a list of ALL persons we have harmed AND become WILLING to make restitution to them. This is a two-fer, you have to do both parts, and to do both parts, it is going to take some more humility among other things.

This verse, Colossians 3:12-13, tells us that now since we are the elect of God (chosen, singled out), we have a task to do. I believe that this is a daily task and that it is essential to this step. We must put on tender mercies, kindness, humility (which we just did), meekness, and longsuffering to complete this step. This is another decision we have to make. God gives us new grace and new mercy every day, and we don't deserve it, so why can't we extend the same to our sisters and brothers? I know it seems like this chapter should be for the other person to read, but it is not, it is specifically for you.

> *Challenge:*
> *Ask the Holy Spirit, while you are on this pitstop of making a list of all the persons you've harmed, to go into your deepest parts and pull out the people you've harmed that you've already buried but have yet to make restitution with them. Who are they? Write those names at the top of your list and seek their forgiveness first.*

God wants our hands and our hearts to be pure and clean. He wants us to be without spot or blemish. God does not want us holding anyone in our hearts or have someone else holding us in theirs. This step is very important and is not to be taken lightly.

For us to even entertain the idea of seeking forgiveness from others, we must have certain characteristics. Some of those characteristics from Colossians 3:12-13 like "tender mercies, kindness, humility, meekness, longsuffering, bearing with one another, and forgiving one another," along with the changes that came with the steps we have completed before, have prepared us to work step 8. This will help us to make an honest, written list of everyone we have harmed and help us to become willing to make restitution to them. Trust me; this is for your good!

You may be saying, "Danika, I did that in step 4 already," but you didn't. Step 4 was about you; this is about the other person. What do I mean? In this part of our journey, we have to take a break and fuel up for the road ahead. Depending on what you did in your addiction and how much harm you caused, this may be a long pit stop — however, a necessary pitstop.

Coming up with this list was a little bit harder than doing my own personal inventory, simply because I refused to believe that I could have caused harm to other people. I was a "good" person. People enjoyed spending time with me and being around me, especially when the liquor was pouring! So how could I, Danika, have harmed someone?! This must be a mistake, I thought, but it wasn't. I was the one who was wrong.

When I started this journey, unpleasant things were revealed to me by the Holy Spirit. Things that I have repressed deep down into my own sea of forgetfulness, but when they were revealed to me, I could not deny them.

One thing, in particular, I will share, was when I realized I was a murderer and was causing death and eternity in Hell, not only upon myself but on to another person as well. Yes, you read right, I was a murderer, and no, I did not have to physically kill someone to get this title, but when I read Proverbs 7, the Word revealed to me that I was a killer.

**Proverbs 7:21-23 reads as follows:**

"With her enticing speech she caused him to yield, with her flattering lips she seduced him. Immediately he went after her, as an ox goes to the slaughter, or as a fool to the correction of the stocks, Till an arrow struck his liver. As a bird hastens to the snare, he did not know it would cost his life."

I knew adultery (being with a married man) wasn't right, but I was in my addiction, and I did not care. I wanted who I wanted, regardless of who had them! So not only was I a murderer, but I was a thief also – coveting. But let's get back on track. When I came to Christ and repented and turned from my wicked ways, adultery was no longer on the table for me, but that wasn't the end. As I got to step

8 and began writing my list, that person's name popped up again. I couldn't figure out why, I just knew I was over it and him, and then I realized I never apologized or even sought forgiveness for the harm I had done, and I could not move on.

Just because I seek forgiveness from another person does not guarantee they will give it to me.

There is one thing you have to keep in mind while working this step. Although you have made your list and became willing to make amends/restitution, you have to keep in mind that the other party may not be receptive, but this is about you and not about them. This is for your journey and the freedom to continue, and that is what this step is about, doing your part. Remember, you cannot control the other person. Just because you seek forgiveness from another does not guarantee they will give it to you. However, you cannot let that deter you.

Now let's talk about this step a little more. You see that after you make your list, you have to become willing to make restitution to those you've harmed. You could make your list and stop there, but really, what good will that do? Seeking forgiveness from others is a powerful thing. It shows that you had a change of heart and a change in your character. It shows that you have realized your wrong and acknowledged your faults. It shows that you have been made new. How amazing is that!?

I'm sure you are not thinking about that, you are probably still saying, "I'll just make my list and leave it there," but can I tell you that list will not let you sleep at night? It will constantly be on and in your heart. Just like the rest of the steps, this one was no mistake, and just like a majority of them, you have a decision to make.

There is just something about forgiveness.

As you write out your list, you will have to decide that no matter what or how long it takes, as long as it does not go against your morals and your beliefs, that you will make restitution with those who will allow you to, because not all may be willing to. However, let me go on the record and say that you do not owe anybody anything

> Depending on the harm that you have caused in your addiction, some things may not be a one-time fix.

BUT God. This is why I said as long as it does not go against your morals and your beliefs. Pray and ask the Holy Spirit to guide you in this process so that people don't take advantage of your vulnerability because they will, but as long as God is leading you and the Holy Spirit is guiding you, you will be able to discern what is right and what is not.

As you complete this step, it will remain with you for the rest of your journey – becoming a part of your character. It will bring you to a place of immediate repentance where you will apologize in that moment of doing someone wrong as opposed to doing it further down the line. I believe this is because once you start down this path of recovery, the feeling of the weights lifting from you is remarkable! There is just something about forgiveness.

> Forgiveness is more than just saying "I'm sorry".

Now, as we move on to Step 9, where we act on our decision to make restitution, keep in mind that everyone may not be receptive and that is okay. This is for your journey to recovery. Forgiveness is more for you than it is for the other person and forgiveness is more than just saying, "I'm sorry."

"Addiction makes you somebody you ain't." - Anonymous

# Chapter 9:
## Restitution and Reconciliation

## Restitution and Reconciliation: "Wherever possible, make direct restitution to all persons you have harmed."[4]

*"Therefore, if you bring your gift to the altar, and there remember that your brother has something against you, leave your gift there before the altar, and go your way. First, be reconciled to your brother, and then come and offer your gift."* - Matthew 5:23-24

Okay, I admit, this could very well be a continuation of chapter 8, but it is not. This chapter is its own entity because this is where the real work takes place. Yes, you have made your list. Great job! Now, are you going to put in the work necessary to continue on this journey?

I do wish some things were as easy as saying, "Father, forgive me" and that's it, but the truth of the matter is, it is not. There are multiple times in the Bible where we see we have to act upon certain things we say. We can't just say stuff; we have to also do stuff.

> *"What does it profit, my brethren, if someone says he has faith but does not have works? Can faith save him? Thus also faith by itself, if it does not have works, is dead."* [33]

This scripture shows us we can't just say we are going to do something or speak things in faith, we also have to do and put some work into it. This, in turn, shows that we are followers/disciples of Christ because our actions will line up with His.

For example, we cannot confess Jesus as our Lord and Savior and continue living the life of a sinner. At that moment when you believe in your heart and confess with your mouth that Jesus died and rose again for your sake and your sins, you have been forgiven, and you have been saved. So how can you be saved and still be living in bondage, sin, and addiction? Riddle me that, Batman.

Now, I don't want to get off topic. I'm very good at that. Step 9 is where the action is. This verse, Matthew 5:23-24, tells us that if we bring our gift to the altar and in that moment, remember that someone has something against us, we are to leave our gift and go our way to FIRST be reconciled with that person and then come back and

---

[33] James 2:14,17

offer our gift. This is deep! We cannot even offer a gift if someone has something against us without first being reconciled with them. So, imagine if it is the other way around and we did something to another person and have not reconciled that situation.

### *How can you be saved and still be living in bondage, sin, and addiction?*

Restitution and reconciliation are simply just to make amends. Meaning, all you are doing is trying to right your wrongs. Sometimes it will be easy, and sometimes it will be hard. Remember in Chapter 7, I spoke about how I lost my mother's trust? Gaining her trust back was not an easy thing. Even when I was telling the truth, she didn't believe me. That was very frustrating! I was doing right, but was still being accused of doing wrong. Has that ever happened to you? Sometimes that will happen during this step and on this journey. Depending on the harm that you've caused in your addiction, some things may not be a one-time fix. Gaining my mom's trust back surely wasn't, but I made it up in my mind that I was willing to make restitution with her. Eventually, I did.

I can honestly say the relief I felt after making restitution was a feeling like none other and that feeling was not contingent upon her forgiving me or not, it was solely because I did my part. This, in turn, became a part of my nature. I find myself thinking twice before I act and although I still fall short, I am now pressed to make restitution as quickly as possible.

As much as you may not like the idea of reconciliation and restitution, it is imperative that you do so. It is a part of the journey to recovery because God knows best. We have to remember and understand that everything is not about us, even on this Christian walk. Although this particular step is to make ourselves free, it is also beneficial for the other person. Just think about how you feel when someone apologizes to you for doing you wrong or causing you harm. Is that not a good feeling? Is that not something you would want to extend to another person?

> We cannot even offer a gift if someone has something against us without first being reconciled with them. Imagine if it is the other way around and we did something to another person and have not reconciled that situation.

In the last chapter, you were given a challenge. In doing this challenge, there should have been some things revealed to you that you may not recall or wish you didn't recall, but now you have. This is what makes this step difficult. It is one thing to admit something to yourself, but it is another thing to admit to others; however, the truth shall set you free. We all have skeletons in our closet that we want to remain buried with us, but some of those skeletons need to be revealed. If they cannot be revealed, you cannot be healed.

### *If it has been brought to your remembrance, you are now responsible to make amends.*

In doing this step, you must make sure you are being led. If it will cause harm to you or the other person, it is best not to make amends directly. Also, keep in mind that this step is only about reconciliation and restitution.

> **If your skeletons cannot be revealed, you cannot be healed.**

It is admitting to the other person the harm that you believe to be true that you caused. Nothing more and nothing less. This step is not to point the finger and say, "I did this because you did that." If you find yourself making amends and pointing the finger while doing so, you are still in addiction, and you need to revisit the previous steps.

This step also does not have a time limit or a time frame. In other words, it could have been revealed that you did something to someone in your early 20s and now you are in your late 40s. This does not disqualify you from making reconciliation or restitution. If it has been brought to your remembrance, you are now responsible to make amends. It may also be a case where the person you have harmed passed away. Again, this does not release you from the obligation of reconciliation. You can make amends indirectly by writing a letter or offering assistance to another person in the same capacity you've harmed the deceased.

Also, if making restitution and reconciliation will cause harm to you or the other person, then the wisest decision would be to make amends from afar or indirectly. This could be writing a letter, journaling, or something along those lines. Sometimes, you may have to think outside the box because it may not be as simple as a phone call or a meetup at the coffee shop. This is a healthy journey, not a harmful journey.

If the other person is confrontational or just not willing to listen to what you have to say, please do not feel compelled to argue your case. Your job is to simply go to that person, acknowledge the harm you have caused, and seek ways to make amends. Keep in mind that some people may try to take advantage of you, but do not let them. You have to make sure you are right with God, not with man.

> ***This is a healthy journey and not a harmful journey.***

For me, a lot of my reconciliation and restitution are accomplished through my spoken word pieces. It is not to take the place of directly making amends, because I have done so, both directly and indirectly. But my writing allows me to keep it in the light and out in the forefront to make sure I remain on the straight and narrow as well as share some of the harm I have caused to others with others so that they too may be offered a push to make restitution and reconciliation. We will get into that more as we continue on this journey. Now, let's move on to Step 10: Daily Accountability.

*Turn right and keep straight."*
*- Anonymous*

## Chapter 10:
## Daily Accountability

## Daily Accountability: "Continue to take personal inventory, and when you are wrong, promptly admit it."[4]

*"I beseech you therefore, brethren, by the mercies of God, that you present your bodies a living sacrifice, holy, acceptable to God, which is your reasonable service. And do not be conformed to this world, but be transformed by the renewing of your mind, that you may prove what is that good and acceptable and perfect will of God."*
*- Romans 12:1-2*

Hello! Welcome to Step 10! If you are still here, you are very serious about recovery, and you are doing great. Not only that, but the rest of the journey may come as a breeze. The first nine steps taught us a new way of living and now it's maintenance time! Daily accountability is holding yourself responsible on a daily basis. Simple enough right? Sometimes, not so much.

The steps of recovery are said to only work if you work them, and you have to work them in order the first time. When we make it to Step 10, it's a continuation of the steps before. We have to continue to take personal inventory, and when we are wrong, we have to admit it promptly. It's not about making another list, but it is about actively checking our hearts and our intentions.

I remember the first time hearing a pastor speak on Romans 12:1-2. I had just started my journey to recovery. I closed up shop (my legs) and put the bottle down, and I was now seeing with new eyes. Little did I know, I was also hearing with new ears. The end of verse one says, "which is your reasonable service;" when

> **This first nine steps taught us a new way of living and now its maintenance time!**

the pastor broke it down, he said, "In other words, this is the least you can do." What you say! See, I was thinking by me not having sex anymore and getting drunk anymore that I was doing God a favor, when all along I was doing what I was supposed to be doing from jump and it was the LEAST I can do! I was floored. However, I appreciated this message because it helped me to hold myself accountable more.

### *It's the least you can do.*

I wish I could say that as the days went by, it got easier, but I can't. At times, even though I was on this road to recovery, there were some hard times. There were times when I didn't want to hold myself accountable, I didn't want to admit when I was wrong, and I definitely didn't want to continue on this journey, but then I was reminded of my sins and my addictions. I then started working the steps even more during those times. I had to be honest with myself. I had to have hope. I had to trust in God even if I didn't understand. I had to be humble. Every day, I have to remind myself not only of the steps, but why I am working the steps, and why I am on this journey in the first place.

> *Honesty moment:*
> *As you continue to take a personal inventory of yourself, are you doing everything you are supposed to be doing?*
> *Are you loving like you should be?*
> *Are you giving like you should be?*
> *Are you walking in humility?*
> *Are you producing good fruits and being Christ-like in your everyday actions?*

As we continue to hold ourselves accountable and continue to take a personal inventory daily, we keep ourselves in the light. We find out things, new things, about ourselves that we need to work on, or even old things that we must continue to work on, and that is the point of this step. It keeps us walking and carrying on. It keeps us on our knees praying. It keeps us in relationship with God.

Step 10 continues to show us that we need God's help and that we cannot continue on this journey on our own. There is this false belief that once you give your life to Christ, you will no longer be subject to trials, hurt, pain, and tribulations. As wonderful as that would be, it is most certainly not the case. It seems as if, once you give your life to Christ, all hell breaks loose! This is not to scare you off, but this is to open your eyes as to why.

> **The minute you give your life to Christ and start on this journey and begin to do right, is the minute the devil realize you are no longer under his control.**

When you are in your addiction (your sin), there is no need for the enemy to attack you; you are his friend and under his control. However, once you decide to turn over a new leaf and live a new life, you are no longer under his control. The devil does not like that. The minute you give your life to Christ and start on this journey and begin to do the right thing is the minute the devil realizes you are no longer under his control. Now he has to try everything in his power to get you back.

When I was sitting in meetings, I heard quite a few stories of how, as soon as a person decided to get clean, the dealer was blowing up their line. Normally, the "junkie" would have to stalk and hound the dealer, but now that the junkie started on his/her journey, the dealer was hounding them down. My fellow brothers and sisters, this is not a coincidence.

Now, I dare not say that my grandfather's death was something of the enemy to try and win me back, but there was another incident that I know was of him.

Before I was completely serious about giving my life to Christ, I had my eyes on this one particular girl. Yes, keep reading. This particular girl was entertaining me, but wasn't really giving me any play. However, a few months along this journey, she gave in to my advances and agreed to go out with me. I wish I could say that I didn't "pick up" by taking her out, but I did. Afterward, I felt all kinds of guilt and shame because I have killed my witness by hooking up with this girl. I played with the thought of just throwing in the towel and giving up, but I remembered Step 1. I remembered that I was powerless over my addiction and my life became unmanageable.

So, what did I do? I started over!! I eventually made restitution and reconciliation with this particular girl and put that in my past. Now, it is a daily task to check my mind, my heart, and my actions, not only about this particular instance but about my life as a whole. I tell you this not to deter you or to make you feel comfortable in doing wrong. When you know better, you do better, and the second time around, I knew better. This is why I am now able to write about the journey.

Now, let's have our honesty moment. As you continue to take a personal inventory of yourself, are you doing everything you are supposed to be doing? Are you loving like you should be? Are you giving like you should be? Are you walking in humility? Are you producing good fruits and being Christ-like in your everyday actions?

Every answer may not be "yes," and every answer may not be "no;" it just may be a mixture of the two, and that is okay. These are some of the things that we should be asking ourselves and considering as we continue on this journey. Every day, we should be striving to be more like Christ. Every day, we should be better than the day before. Every day, we should be checking ourselves to make sure we are right in the sight of God.

# ONE STEP AT A TIME:

## *The ending destination of this journey is to reunite with our Father in Heaven.*

This step is very important. So important that the Bible even tells us to examine ourselves before we partake in the Lord's Supper (Communion).

*"But let a man examine himself, and so let him eat of the bread and drink of the cup. For he who eats and drinks in an unworthy manner eats and drinks judgment to himself, not discerning the Lord's body.[34]"*

This examination or accountability should be daily, not just on Communion Sunday. If you don't hold yourself accountable daily, here, while you are on earth, you will most definitely regret it when you step foot in front of the Judge because you will be held accountable for sure then.

Each day, I pray and tell the Lord, "Lord, search me." Not because I know that I am wrong or that I have done wrong, but because I don't want to be found in the wrong. I hope that made sense. And every day, you must take an

---

[34] 1 Corinthians 11:28-29

inventory of yourself, and if you find any faults or any wrongs, you must admit it immediately. This is what will keep you clean, this is what will keep you pure, and this is what will keep you humble to continue on this journey.

On this journey, I want to be able to help others, and I cannot fully do that if I am in addiction, if my hands are dirty, or if I am trying to hide stuff. This is why you keep things in the light and have a repentant heart. It is my prayer that after reading this chapter, you would be reminded of that humility you've obtained in Chapter 7 to keep you humbled enough to promptly say, "I'm sorry for my wrong actions." By doing so, you hold yourself accountable while releasing that pain or person from your heart.

It will be so much easier to continue the journey to our ending destination without that weight, and in case you were wondering, the ending destination of this journey is to reunite with our Father in Heaven.

*"If you don't pick up, you won't get loaded."*
*- Anonymous*

# Chapter 11:
## Personal Revelation

## Personal Revelation: "Seek through prayer and meditation to know the Lord's will and to have the power to carry it out."[4]

*"This Book of the Law shall not depart from your mouth, but you shall meditate in it day and night, that you may observe to do according to all that is written in it. For then you will make your way prosperous, and then you will have good success."* - Joshua 1:8

Do you want to have '*good success*' in Recovery? If the answer is "yes," then you need to have a personal revelation. Step 11, I believe, is the answer to "Why Recovery?" A personal revelation will keep you focused on the journey ahead; it will keep you clean and sober, and it will help you live a holy and righteous life. A personal revelation makes "Why Recovery" relatable and real to the individual. One thing about recovery is, you cannot do it for others, you have to do it for yourself.

At first, I thought Step 11 was about purpose to go out and be of service to others, which does help prepare you for the next step; but then I realized Step 11 is purposed for me personally and it is personally purposed for you too. Reason being, a personal revelation helps you be successful in recovery because when you are very confident about something, you will not be easily shaken, like the wise man who built his house on the rock.

*"Therefore, whoever hears these sayings of Mine, and does them, I will liken him to a wise man who built his house on the rock:, and the rain descended, the floods came, and the winds blew and beat on that house; and it did not fall, for it was founded on the rock."*[35]

The wise man is someone who hears the sayings of the Lord (seeking through prayer and meditation on the Lord's will) and does them (carry it out). The "rock" signifies God's will and His Word. When we build and live our lives according to God's will and His Word, when the rain descends, the floods come, and the winds blow and beat in our lives, we will not fall! So how will I know the Lord's will? By prayer and meditation.

Prayer is simply a means of communication between you and God. God is always there with a listening ear, ready and waiting on you to arrive. Also, communication is a two-

---

[35] Matthew 7:24-25

way street. One speaks, and the other one listens and vice versa.

> *Stop and ponder:*
> *What is your "Why?"*
> *Why are you on this road to recovery?*
> *Why now?*
> *Why were you saved?*

It may be hard to believe, but God wants to talk back to you as well. How else would you know His will if 1) You don't ask Him and 2) He doesn't tell you? The personal revelation you receive from the Lord will shift your focus and help you see things clearer. At one point, your focus was on your addiction, and that's what motivated a lot of your actions, but now, your focus is on doing the will of the Father.

## *You cannot do it for others; you have to do it for yourself.*

When I recommitted my life to Christ in 2013, I felt the shift, and I started to think and feel differently. I stopped having the desire to engage in certain conversations. I no longer wanted to hang out until the late hours of the night drinking.

I became easily agitated with peers who were talking about things with no purpose, and I got talked about. Yep. I kept hearing the phrase, "It is not that serious" over and over again and sometimes, I was told, "You need to loosen up;" however, I knew why my recovery was important and what I needed to do to stay on the road to recovery.

> **If you are on the fence with remaining sober or living for Christ, you are at high risk for relapse or backsliding.**

I say that to say, the Lord's will is going to set you apart and no matter how supportive or unsupportive your support system is, if you are on the fence with remaining sober or living for Christ, you are at high risk for relapse or backsliding. However, when you are very confident about something, you will not be easily shaken. Plus, once you have something deep down in your spirit, it will be hard to convince you of anything otherwise, because after all, "*A double minded man is unstable*

> **God wants to talk back to you as well.**

*in all his ways."*[36]

Now, let's get into this meditation. The key scripture for this chapter says, *"meditate in it day and night."* "It" is the Word of God. When you meditate on something, you are constantly thinking about it. Therefore, if we are to meditate on the Word of God day and night, then we are to think about the Word of God constantly. In return, this will give us *"good success."*

This does not necessarily mean reading the Bible all day and night, but it's keeping the Word of God in our remembrance and carrying it out. *"But be doers of the word, and not hearers only, deceiving yourselves."*[37] In addition, we should also be constantly thinking about the twelve steps and constantly working the steps. We do this by going to meetings, going to church, and revisiting previous steps when necessary. Therefore, when temptation arises, or those urges and cravings creep back in, you will not fall like the wise man because of the personal revelation you received!

Again, the steps are designed to work in order for a reason. Step 11 is one step further than Step 10, and it is to

---

[36] James 1:8

[37] James 1:22

help prepare you for Step 12. Personal Revelation helps you to continue to be honest, increase your hope, and strengthen your trust in God. It helps you to continue to seek truth and make confessions; it constantly changes your heart and brings you to humility to seek forgiveness. It allows you to reconcile swiftly as you hold yourself accountable daily. Personal revelation provides you with the answer to "Why recovery," so that when others in bondage see you walking freely, and they wonder, or they ask you, "How," you can answer them, without a shadow of a doubt, which brings us to our last step: Service.

*"Don't jump in a car unless you have a destination."* - Anonymous

## Chapter 12:

*Service*

## Service: "Having a spiritual awakening as a result of the Atonement of Jesus Christ, share this message with others and practice these principles in all you do."[4]

*"However, Jesus did not permit him, but said to him, 'Go home to your friends, and tell them what great things the Lord has done for you, and how He has had compassion on you.' And he departed and began to proclaim in Decapolis all that Jesus had done for him, and all marveled."*
*- Mark 5:19-20*

Wow! You have made it to the end of this journey. Congratulations! Well, I take that back, you have officially made it back to the beginning. The steps are not to complete 1-12 and then stop as if it is over. The steps are to be completed continuously. As long as you have breath in your body, you should be working the steps. The only thing that should have changed is your starting point. We started in our addiction (sins) and are leaving them behind. Now we are continuing in the newness of life. Walking as the new creations that we are. That right there is a journey within itself!

*Service puts deliverance on the forefront and problems on the back burner.*

This chapter is on service. While preparing to write this chapter, I realized that service brings upon four "S" words that we humans typically do not like.

**Those words are:**
- Surrender
- Sacrifice
- Submission
- Self-LESS-ness

Each of these words, including service, challenge you to place another person above yourself. I have come to a place in my journey where I stumbled at service, due to my own selfishness. I have found myself in the "woe is me" line instead of the "He did this for me" line. You see, service puts deliverance on the forefront and problems on the back burner, and if you are like me and stumble at service, that means your perception is off.

*But what about the others who are lost in sin and drowning in their addictions?*

Once you get saved (*confess with your mouth the Lord Jesus and believe in your heart that God has raised Him from the dead*[38]), you <u>surrender</u> your life to Christ, <u>sacrificing</u> your will and your way, <u>submitting</u> to His authority, and thinking <u>less of yourself</u>, resulting in true service. I have learned through many occasions that I cannot truly serve the Lord or others or provide service if I am caught up in myself. Being caught up in self, to me, equates to being caught up in addictions (sins) and when we are caught up in addictions (sins), it is all about us.

When we are caught up in self, we have a "give me 'me'" mentality. It's all about "when is *my* next score," "where is *my* next drink," "who is *my* next victim," "my, my, my." However, the first step tells us our lives have become unmanageable, and it's obvious to me that being caught up in self is not the mindset and perspective we should have. When you accept Jesus and have Him in your life, you change. Everything about you changes. Your heart changes, your mind changes, your actions change, your demeanor changes! However, this change doesn't happen overnight.

---

[38] Romans 10:9

Regarding service, my Elect Lady, Wency Casby (Full Life Faith Ministries, Marrero, LA), often says, "Give to others what you wish was given to you. When I first heard her say it, I didn't quite get what she meant, but I put it in my mental bank and kept on living. But as I continued along this journey, I realized that phrase alone talks all about service, whether the act is big or small.

For Elect Lady Casby, her service is hugs (among many other things). The best ones at that! She stated (and I am paraphrasing) that she desired hugs as a youth and wasn't getting them, so that's why she gives hugs: *"Give to others what you wish was given to you."* Her hugs are so tender and pure. I can only believe that comes from her love for Christ.

> ***Don't you wish someone was there to tell you what they have been through in hopes that you didn't have to go through the same?***

To serve someone in true capacity, you must die to yourself. Don't let me lose you, let me show you. Elect Lady was not receiving hugs as a child, so if she never received hugs, especially tender and pure hugs, how does she know how to give them? I'll tell you, death! She could have said, "Well, nobody gave me hugs, why should I give hugs?" But she had a spiritual awakening as an atonement of Jesus Christ, and she started to share her message with others and practice those principles in all that she does. A true example of service!

One thing I have learned about **true** service is that it is a hard thing! If you look at Jesus' life, the thirty-three years He lived and walked this earth (minus the few years the Bible does not talk about), you will see that Jesus lived a life of service. His main purpose for being born was to serve us sinners by dying the worst possible death one can even imagine (Reference John 3:16-17)! However, that is true service: DYING! Dying to self and that is no easy task. This is where the spiritual awakening comes into play.

"Spiritual awakening" is an important factor in service. When God is revealed to you, it goes beyond what the mind can receive because it doesn't make sense. The mind cannot grasp the concept of a man dying and rising again three days later, but the spirit can. Our spirit man can relate because we were once dead to our sins, but once we received Jesus as our Lord and Savior and confessed that He died and rose again, we too rose again. This revelation is what helps us to go and tell it on the mountain. Unashamedly.

## *Jesus didn't save you for you.*

This journey, your journey, is for others as much as it is for you. While on this Christian journey and road to recovery, I've realized that Jesus not only saved me for me, Jesus saved me to help others as well. Once I received that personal revelation, I became equipped to serve others by sharing the gospel and my testimony of how the Lord brought me out of darkness. These steps bring about change which, in return, helps us to provide service to others. So yeah, you got saved and became sober because that's what you needed for yourself, but what about the others who are lost in sin and drowning in their addictions?

When I first recommitted my life to Christ, I was all excited to tell people about the goodness of Jesus and all that He has done for me. It was exciting, and I wanted to share my excitement with everyone else so that they too can experience what I experienced. In the beginning, it was blissful. Heck, in the beginning, it was easy. However, as I continued along on this journey, I realized that sharing the gospel with others is not as easy as I thought it was going to be. Not everyone will be receptive to hear what you have to say and if they do listen, not many will receive what I have to say, and that is okay; our job is to share the message and practice in all that we do!

Now, let me have an honest moment. We know that not everyone is easy to love, yet we are commanded to love one another as Christ loves us[39] and Christ loves us unto death. I am not there yet! For that reason, I say true service is dying. When I can put myself and my feelings aside, I will be able to serve others better. However, sometimes I am still in the forefront, and that is what hinders me from true service.

---

True service =
1. Surrendering your life to Christ.
2. Sacrificing your will and your way.
3. Submitting to His authority.
4. Thinking less of yourself.

---

When I am in the front, I cannot serve God properly. I cannot serve my husband properly. I cannot serve others properly and neither can you. In those moments, you have to take a step back and examine yourself. Daily accountability, remember?

---

[39] John 13:34-35

## *Service keeps you clean.*

Each day you arise in your right mind and serve the Lord with your life and actions, you are a living and walking testimony. Your life should be a life of service, whether it's verbally or non-verbally because this is a verbal (share this message) and non-verbal (practice these principles in all that you do) step. Others should be able to look at you and know that you are a disciple (follower) of Christ, even if they never hear you say it out of your mouth, and that can happen by the way that we serve. *"By this, all will know that you are My disciples if you have love for one another."*[40]

Service is important because service is what will help keep you and I on track with this journey, and I believe it is no coincidence that the steps end with service because service keeps you clean. Service, according to dictionary.com, is simply, "an act of helpful activity; help; aid."[41] A form of service as it relates to substance abuse is becoming a sponsor. A sponsor, in a spiritual sense, is a

---

[40] John 13:35

[41] Service. (n.d.). *Dictionary.com Unabridged.* Retrieved from http://www.dictionary.com/browse/service

mentor. By being a sponsor or spiritual mentor, you are giving back to someone and aiding them in their road to recovery.

Another form of service is community service. An earthly judge may often sentence or order someone to do community service hours for committed offenses. The services are mostly related to the offense they committed. For instance, giving speeches to school children about the dangers of drunk driving for a person convicted of driving under the influence (DUI).[42] Although it may seem that the community is benefiting from service performed, it is expected that the individual is gaining insight on his or her offense as well. So you see, naturally and spiritually, service doesn't just help others, it helps us too.

As a believer, service is an important factor in your walk with Christ. Remember the Great Commission we were called to do? *"Go therefore and make disciples of all the nations, baptizing them in the name of the Father and of the Son and of the Holy Spirit, teaching them to observe all*

---

[42] Court Ordered Community Service. Retrieved from https://criminal.findlaw.com/criminal-procedure/court-ordered-community-service.html

things that I have commanded you; and lo, I am with you always, even to the end of the age. Amen."[43]

We have to go out and share what God has done for us to others. In this journey, we have to help others. We have to share what God has done for us so that others may receive the same. We must also "be fruitful and multiply," and that's not just talking about birthing babies in the natural! We should also be birthing babies in the spirit and multiplying the Kingdom!

Service doesn't have to be this gigantic, grand gesture. Service can be something as small as a hug like Elect Lady. It may seem small to you, but you never know the size of the seed you're planting or the amount of water you are giving to the person on the receiving end. People are dying, and we need to get them saved! We must share our message with others and practice these principles in all that we do! Service.

**I am a product of someone's service.**

---

[43] Matthew 28:19-20

"Recovery is a service. Give it to others because someone gave it to you and it doesn't cost you nothing but time."
-Anonymous

# Conclusion

## ONE STEP AT A TIME: CONCLUSION

Each step you take, beginning at Step 1, is a continuous learning process. You may even have to learn how to be honest to start your journey, and that is okay. God is with you every step of the way. God is there with you through honesty, hope, trust in God, truth, confession, change of heart, humility, seeking forgiveness, restitution and reconciliation, daily accountability, personal revelation, and service. The very fact that you have God on your side means you already have the upper hand to be freed from your sins and addictions.

While completing this book, I was challenged, discouraged, tempted, and felt like a true failure. The only thing that kept me going, other than the grace of God, was admitting to myself that I, alone, was powerless over my addictions; which came in the form of procrastination and delayed obedience. After I was honest with myself and I put God in the forefront, my hope was restored. My trust in God strengthened. I was able to combat lies and "stinking thinking" with the truth, and I confessed my wrongdoings to those I harmed. That, in turn, gave me not only a change of heart, but an attitude change that caused me to walk in humility and seek forgiveness, restitution, and reconciliation from myself.

Once I was able to recognize my shortcomings and forgive myself and make amends, I was able to hold myself accountable daily by keeping my personal revelation in my mind and constantly reminding myself that this book is my service and it needs to be shared with others. Working the steps completed this book – literally, "*One Step at a Time.*"

I say that to let you know, dear reader, that there are times when you are going to slip and may even fall, but you don't have to stay down. Recovery is real. Salvation is real. Your sins can be forgiven and washed away, and you can live as a new creation in Christ, but you have to take that first step. Jesus already did His part on Calvary when He died for our sins. The move is now on you. Keep in mind, the steps only work if you work them!

It is my prayer that this book inspires, challenges, convicts, and creates such urgency in you to give your life to Christ and be set free from addictions and sin. If you're already in Christ, I pray this book encourages you to continue walking on the straight and narrow while providing you with all the tools to help you along the way – one step at a time.

Bless and Be Blessed!
Danika Kayelle XOXO

www.ingramcontent.com/pod-product-compliance
Lightning Source LLC
Chambersburg PA
CBHW071453070526
44578CB00001B/329